W9-CDY-719

HARRIER

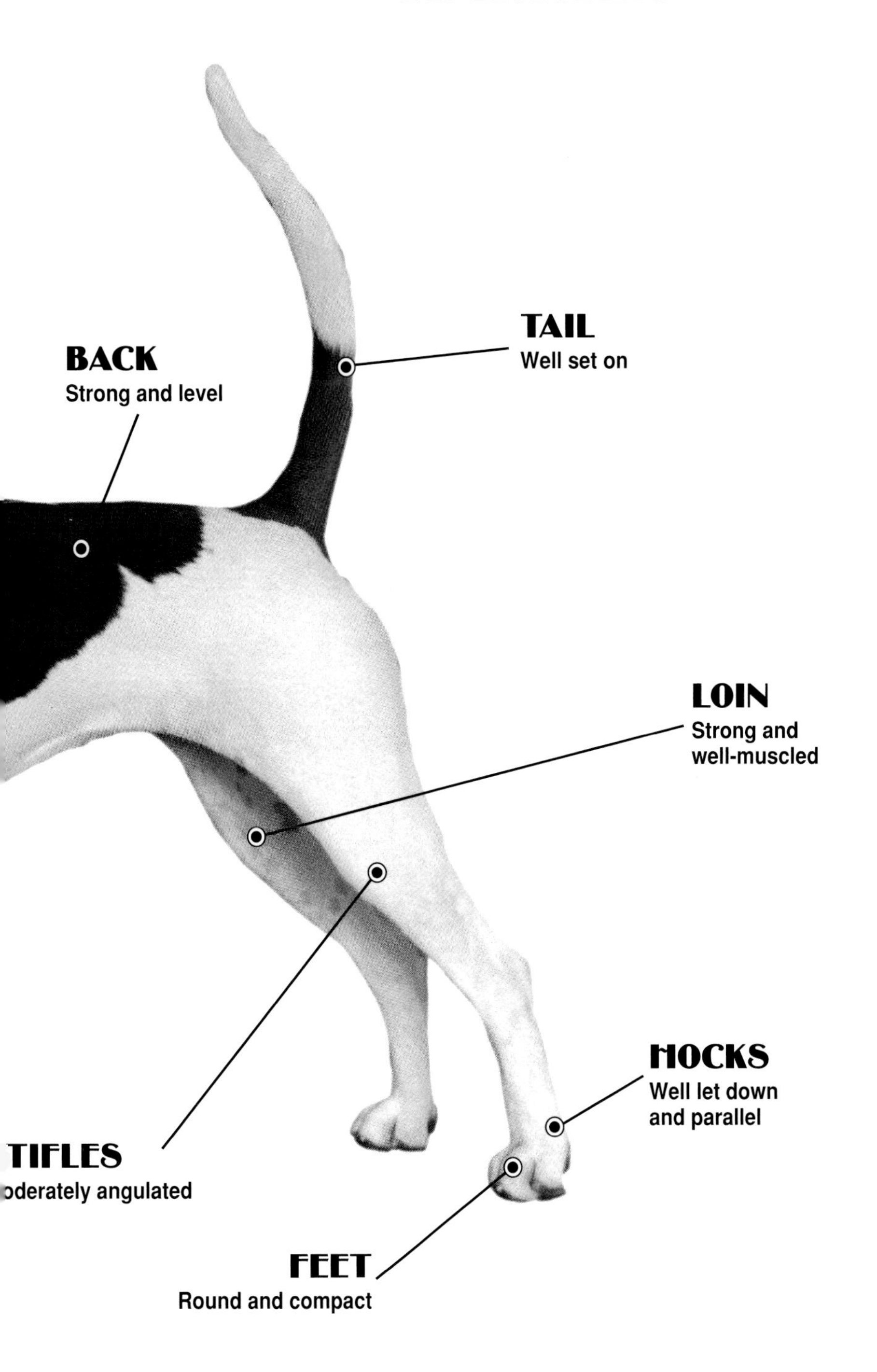
TAIL
Well set on
BACK
Strong and level
LOIN
Strong and
well-muscled
HOCKS
Well let down
and parallel
TIFLES
oderately angulated
FEET
Round and compact

Title Page: High Peak Harrier Pack of England

Photographers: A. E. Keil-Wizard Imagery, Donna Smiley-Auborn and John Auborn, Rich Bergman, Betty Burnell, Jim Densmore, Isabelle Francais, Kathryn Martel, Mikron Photos, Kim Mitchell, Julie Wright

Distributed in the UNITED STATES to the Pet Trade by T.F.H. Publications, Inc., 1 TFH Plaza, Neptune City, NJ 07753; on the Internet at www.tfh.com; in CANADA by Rolf C. Hagen Inc., 3225 Sartelon St., Montreal, Quebec H4R 1E8; Pet Trade by H & L Pet Supplies Inc., 27 Kingston Crescent, Kitchener, Ontario N2B 2T6; in ENGLAND by T.F.H. Publications, PO Box 74, Havant PO9 5TT; in AUSTRALIA AND THE SOUTH PACIFIC by T.F.H. (Australia), Pty. Ltd., Box 149, Brookvale 2100 N.S.W., Australia; in NEW ZEALAND by Brooklands Aquarium Ltd., 5 McGiven Drive, New Plymouth, RD1 New Zealand; in SOUTH AFRICA by Rolf C. Hagen S.A. (PTY.) LTD., P.O. Box 201199, Durban North 4016, South Africa; in JAPAN by T.F.H. Publications, Japan—Jiro Tsuda, 10-12-3 Ohjidai, Sakura, Chiba 285, Japan. Published by T.F.H. Publications, Inc.

MANUFACTURED IN THE
UNITED STATES OF AMERICA
BY T.F.H. PUBLICATIONS, INC.

HARRIER

A COMPLETE AND RELIABLE HANDBOOK

John Auborn & Donna Smiley-Auborn
& Kathryn Martel

RX-127

HISTORY OF THE HARRIER

Hunting hare with hounds is a very ancient sport. Xenophon wrote of keeping a pack and hunting in ancient Greece. He also described the qualities of a good hound and how to hunt the hare. While his general description could fit the Harrier—the Romans brought hounds to England—the breed, as we know it today, is likely a product of slightly more recent breeding.

The Normans were the first to keep records of hounds in England, and it is known that they had brought their own hounds with them after invading the country. The first recorded pack in England was the Pennistone Pack, which was owned by Midas De Midhope in 1260 and was kept together for over 500 years. The Holcombe Harriers, still hunting today, are chronicled in a visit of King James I to their hunting territory in 1617.

Often the subject of sporting artwork and prints, a pack of hounds is a familiar image, whether Harriers, Foxhounds, or Beagles. Indeed, the three breeds are closely related and their bloodlines have often been mixed in efforts to share the best of each. Harriers were originally hunted on foot. As mounted fox hunting became more fashionable in the 18th and 19th centuries, more foxhound blood was introduced and faster Harriers developed.

In March of 1891, the Association of Masters of Harriers and Beagles (AMHB) was formed and published a stud book. The volumes of 1891-1900 listed 107 registered packs of Harriers and 40 Beagle packs. The group also began to run the Peterborough Harrier and Beagle Show in 1892. Records of Peterborough Shows and photos of the winners are published annually in the stud book. Admission of the foundation stock for the 1891 edition was based on either individual pack records or by committee. A committee continually admitted hounds for several years. Many of these "foundation" Harriers were, in fact, small Foxhounds with parents from recognized Foxhound kennels. Some of the foundation Harriers appear in top-winning Beagle pedigrees, so "Harrier" often defined the type of hunting and size of hound rather than pedigree in early AMHB packs. The practice of interbreeding with Foxhounds still occurs in England and is reflected in the pedigrees kept by the AMHB. Some claim today's Harriers are nothing more than small Foxhounds, but their history and a good percentage of their bloodlines prove differently.

The West Country Harrier is a strain with claims to more ancient Harrier blood. Several packs did not breed to the Foxhound-type or stud-book Harriers of the AMHB packs. They were able to remain separate until World War I, but they joined AMHB in 1927 and added their own "West Country Pure Harrier" section to the stud books.

Dwindling bloodlines and World War II put an end to exclusive breeding, but a different type of Harrier remained. Today, most of the West Country packs have larger, lighter-colored hounds and hunt foxes exclusively, yet still claim to be the purer Harrier type. Traditional packs are still active and found in England, Ireland, Australia, and New Zealand.

This 1894 photo depicts the Clifton Foot Harriers of the United Kingdom with Captain Davis, the Hunt Secretary.

The Harrier is a hardy breed that can hunt in any type of weather or environment. Huntsman Eugene Mackay and the Vale of Lune Pack wait patiently in the rain for the start of a hunt.

HARRIERS IN THE UNITED STATES

Several sources mention "colonial" imports of Harriers. The first specific reference found is from the first entry of the Craven pack in the first AMHB Stud Book. The Craven history mentions Harriers being shipped to America in the 18th century. Unfortunately, it does not specify where these dogs were shipped. These early Harrier imports were undoubtedly used for hunting and crossed with other hounds to create some of our American hound breeds, but their lines do not trace to current Harriers in the US. Lacking the European hare for which the Harrier was developed, hunting in America turned to fox, raccoon, and other game.

In the early 1900s, European hares were brought from Belgium and Austria to establish sustaining populations in New Jersey and New York. Several packs of Harriers hunting in the traditional English style were established early in the 20th century, and many were recognized by the Masters of Foxhounds Association of America. The largest was the pack of 50 couples that belonged to Oakleigh Thorne of Millbrook, New York. The Millbrook pack hunted both hares and foxes and was said to have outperformed the pack of Foxhounds also in residence. Other notable and formalized US packs hunting with Harriers include the Cobbler, Mill Creek, Mr. Seth Thomas's

Opposite: Although there are no Harriers hunting in today's registered US packs, some enthusiasts still hunt with smaller farm packs, privately held packs that are not formally registered with the hunt organizations. Author John Auborn readies his Kingsbury farm pack for hunting.

(now Spring Valley), Dilwyne, Mr. Huntington's, Halfred Farms, Highland, Hilltowns, Aiken, Longmeadow, Mr. Reynal's, and Wayne-Dupage.

The Monmouth County Harriers hunted from the 1930s to the late 1960s in central New Jersey. The hunt still wears green coats, appropriate for Harriers. The Aiken and the Wayne-Dupage packs tried drag hunting (hunting a scented lure trailed by a runner) with their Harriers. The rest hunted European hare, jackrabbit, or fox.

The Nantucket Harriers and the Whiteoakes were started from large Beagles and called "American Harriers." Mr. Clucas, after hunting the Whiteoakes Beagles in New Jersey for 25 years, found that his advancing age required a better way to follow the hounds. In 1932, he mounted the hunt staff on horses and changed the name to Whiteoakes Harriers. The Beagles were bred to Harriers and eventually even to English Foxhounds during the war years. The Nantucket Harriers were hunted on the island in the summertime, providing a unique chance to hunt in July. About ten percent of the current Harrier bloodlines in the US trace back to the formal US packs, the rest to more recent imports from England.

The last formal (registered) Harrier packs in the US disbanded or converted to Foxhounds in the late 1960s. There are occasional Harriers bred into some of the formal Foxhound packs, but none hunt presently in the large registered packs in the US. In California, author John Auborn and his wife, Donna, work their Kingsbury Harriers as a mounted farm pack after jackrabbits, while in Michigan, author Kathryn Martel has her Sunnystone Harriers working as a foot pack (also a farm pack). A farm pack is a small, privately held pack that is not formally registered with the hunt organizations. It is anticipated that with the growing knowledge base and quality imports from England, more Harrier farm packs may be established in the US. Additionally, in New England and in northern Michigan, Harriers are being used to hunt snowshoe hare. The Harrier's size and stamina have been proven to outperform the more commonly used Beagles in the deep snow, yet they are not so big as to be stuck in the brush and thickets. The hunters use shotguns, and the hare is shot while the hounds are trailing their quarry. This type of hunting is markedly different than traditional methods with Harriers and shows the flexibility of this hound.

Harrier Club of America

Founded in 1992, the Harrier Club of America (HCA) is the parent breed club for the American Kennel Club (AKC). Although the AKC has registered Harriers since 1885, no parent breed club was recognized by the AKC until recently, despite at least two prior attempts in the late 1960s and early 1980s.

Information about the 1960s version of the HCA is limited. It was incorporated and had George Schmidt of Paramus, NJ, as Secretary; Ed Johnson and John Schwartz were members. This group was mentioned at least twice in *Popular Dogs* magazine and hoped to have its own shows and field trials.

From 1979 to 1984, a small group of owners and breeders operated independently, again with the name "Harrier Club of America" and shared information within a newsletter, *The Harrier*. They announced their formation/incorporation with an advertisement in *Dog World* magazine. This group supported several shows in Ravenna, Ohio, but lapsed after several years and never obtained AKC status or support. Several former members are part of the present HCA.

In October of 1991, a show in Arizona brought together many Harrier owners who sponsored three days over a weekend of breed trophies under the name "Harrier Fanciers of America." Shortly afterwards, the AKC contacted many breeders to participate in filming the AKC Harrier breed video. This filming resulted in the formal re-creation of the present Harrier Club of America on May 9, 1992, in Lionville, Pennsylvania. At that first meeting, officers were elected and basic rules were formulated, and the club has operated continuously since.

From the beginning, the present HCA was designed to be a national club. Regional directors are selected from three geographic regions—east, midwest, and west. Club activities began with a quarterly newsletter and club-supported entries. Breed information booths have been present at supported shows since 1992. An information pamphlet with the AKC breed standard and useful information about the Harrier was written and is given out by members and at information booths. A judges' packet detailing the Harrier is used at judging seminars, along with giving prospective judges hands-on experience with the dogs.

The HCA offers breed rescue for Harriers with discipline problems or from unsuitable homes. A hunting certification for beginning hounds is in the works, along with a code of ethics for breeders. A website with detailed information can be found at http://www.harriers.net/harriers/HCA.html.

Availability of the Harrier in the US

Harriers are one of the rarest AKC-recognized breeds. To illustrate this, in all of 1994 there were only four Harrier litters born in the entire US, resulting in just 31 puppies. So, if you are seriously considering a Harrier as a pet, please be aware that you may have to wait awhile to find one—you will not be able to go out next weekend and simply get one! Do not expect to find a breeder near you. There are only a handful of breeders across the US, and litters are few and far between. It is best to find a breeder that you feel comfortable with and ask to be put on their waiting list for puppies. Good breeders will also refer you to other breeders upon request. Contact the Harrier Club of America for a listing of breeders that have signed their extensive Code of Ethics, as this is the best way to find a reputable breeder that is committed to the health and welfare of the breed.

Harriers are one of the rarest American Kennel Club recognized breeds in the United States. This group photo is of the Dunston Pack from eastern England.

If you are willing to consider an adult instead of a

puppy, breeders sometimes have adults that are in need of homes, too. These will normally either be retired show dogs that do not fit into their breeding program or grown-up pups that have been returned to the breeder by their original owner. The advantages to adults are that most are housetrained and are past the destructive puppy stage. Furthermore, the costs associated with the acquisition of an older dog are usually a fraction of that of a puppy. Harriers are also occasionally available for adoption through the HCA Rescue Program; visit the Rescue site on the Internet to see if any are currently looking for homes: http://www.harriers.net/harriers/rescue.html.

HARRIER RESCUE

As mentioned previously, Harrier Rescue (a part of the Harrier Club of America, Inc.) exists to help Harriers that are in trouble. Occasionally, they are found in animal shelters, but the majority of dogs are surrendered to the rescue group by their owners when they can no longer care for the hound. The reasons for this vary—behavior problems or a change in the home situation (i.e., a divorce or forced move to an apartment) are the most common. If there are behavior problems, Harrier Rescue first tries to work with the owners to overcome or solve the problems. Should this be ineffective or if the family is unwilling to make the effort, the hound is then brought into an HCA foster home.

The foster home diagnoses behavior problems, works to retrain the hound and solve his problems, and ensures that the hound is in good physical condition, current on vaccinations, and spayed or neutered. The foster home also evaluates the hound to determine what would be the best type of adoptive situations for that individual (i.e., with older children, without cats, with other dogs, etc.).

Prospective adopters must complete a questionnaire to determine their requirements and suitability for a Harrier and must agree to a home inspection prior to placement. Adopters are also required to sign a contract with the HCA that is intended to protect the dog and guarantee that it will be well cared for. Adoption fees, normally much less than the purchase price of a new puppy, cover the expenses involved in the rescue (veterinary care, food, shipping expenses to get the hound to the foster home, etc.), and are quite a bargain.

had special exhibition classes for packs of Foxhounds, Beagles, and Harriers, where hunt staff showed the hounds as a full pack. Horn-blowing contests and other events kept a clear connection to the hunting heritage. In 1936, Ch. Mr. Reynal's Monarch became the first AKC Harrier Champion, won Best American-bred in Show at the WKC show, and defeated 3,751 dogs for an impressive Best in Show at Morris and Essex Kennel Club.

In the early 1960s, a few Harriers began to appear again at AKC shows. In 1965, an impressive entry of Harriers appeared at the Bryn Mawr Hound Show, although there were not enough present for an entry in 1966. Also in 1965, Breezewood Chop Chop became the second AKC Champion of Record after a gap of three decades. Competition was hard to find and most Harriers had to win the Hound Group to earn points. At least two Harriers won Groups, but never compiled enough points to complete their championships.

In 1969, Nabeho's Harvey won Best in Show at Superstition Kennel Club, earning five points towards his championship. In 1970, there were two Best in Show winners, with Ch. Lady Elizabeth of Byron Mews and Ch. Johnson's Pretty Boy Floyd. In 1978, Brentcliffe Jill repeated Harvey's trick, earning five championship points with Best in Show at Janesville-Belloit Kennel Club. She went on to become the all-time winning Harrier with 17 Bests in Show and 52 Hound Group wins. Show activity has continued consistently, in small numbers, ever since.

In 1995, the HCA sponsored an entry of 29 Harriers in Las Vegas, Nevada, and more than 35 were exhibited together in California in 1998. In 1996, Ch. Kingsbury Pacific Ring of Fire broke an 18-year dry spell and won Best in Show at Bayou Kennel Club. Coincidentally, Ch. Pacific's The Edge won Best in Show later that same day! While the majority of Harriers are located in California, there are significant numbers of this breed in Michigan, Washington, Oregon, Arizona, and North Carolina.

In AKC performance events, several Harriers have earned obedience titles, and the breed can even boast about being awarded tracking and agility titles, too.

HARRIERS IN CANADA

Harriers first appeared in the 1891-92 Canadian

Kennel Club Stud Book. There is a photo recording an entire English pack being shipped to Toronto in the 1920s. The Harrier Club of America has only three Canadian members, but the breed has done well in the show ring. Ch. Johnson's Pretty Boy Floyd twice won CKC Best in Show. At the Show of Shows, he won the Hound Group and was the top Canadian Hound for 1970. After more than two decades of little activity, Am. Can. Ch. Kingsbury's Sweet Desert Fire, Am. CD, arrived in Canada in 1996 and became a multi-Best in Show and Group winner. Beginning in 1997, Can. Ch. Wesford Silent Legacy has also been a consistent winner with many Bests in Show and Group wins.

Am. Can. Mex. Int. Ch. Kingsbury's Sweet Desert Fire, CD, bred and owned by author Donna Smiley Auborn and co-owned by Kevin Shupenia, is the top-winning Harrier in Canadian Kennel Club history.

DESCRIPTION OF THE HARRIER

Today's Harrier is a sturdily built, medium-sized dog of impeccable character and temperament. This breed of dog is active, well balanced (both mentally and physically), and full of strength. The Harrier is expected to work tirelessly throughout the day and return home at night to take his place as a loyal and loving companion. As a point of reference, the Harrier is a smaller version of the English Foxhound, rather than a larger version of the Beagle.

The Harrier stands 19 to 21 inches at the shoulder, but a variation of one inch in either direction is acceptable. Generally, males are larger than females. The Harrier's proportion is "off-square." This means that the Harrier is slightly longer than he is tall. He is a solidly built dog, full of strength and quality. This breed has as much substance and bone as possible without being heavy or coarse.

The Harrier's head is in proportion to the overall dog. No part of the head should stand out relative to the other parts. His expression is gentle when relaxed, yet alert when aroused. Eyes are medium sized, set well apart, and brown or hazel in darker dogs, lighter hazel to yellow in lighter dogs, though the darker colors are always desired. The saying that the "eyes are the window to the soul" is certainly an appropriate description of the Harrier. The ears, which are rounded at the tips, are low set and lie close to the cheeks. They are moderately thick and have the texture of velvet.

The skull is in proportion to the entire animal, with good length and breadth and a bold foreface. The muzzle from stop to tip of nose is approximately the

The Harrier is a solidly built dog, full of strength and quality, possessing as much substance as possible without being heavy or coarse.

same length as the stop to the occiput. The muzzle is substantial with good depth, and the lips complete the square, clean look of the muzzle, without excess skin or flews. A good nose is essential. It must be wide, with well-opened nostrils. Teeth meet in a scissors bite or they may be level. Undershot or overshot bites are faulted in the show ring to the degree of the severity of the misalignment.

The Harrier's neck is long and strong with no excess skin or throatiness, sweeping smoothly into the muscling of the forequarters. The topline is level. The back is muscular with no dip behind the withers or roach (or rise, as it is also referred) over the loin, like that of the American Foxhound. In England, a moderate rise over the loin is preferred as it is thought to provide added flexibility to the Harrier's back. Such flexibility is necessary to jump tall walls and hedges, as well as handle the sharp turns of the hare while hunting. The Harrier's chest is deep, extending to the elbows, with well-sprung ribs that extend well back, providing plenty of heart and lung room. The ribs should not be so well sprung that they interfere with the free, efficient, movement of the front assembly.

Opposite: The Harrier expression is gentle when relaxed, but immediately becomes alert and aware when on the scent.

The loin is short, wide, and well muscled.

The long, high tail set of the Harrier is an accurate barometer of his attitude. It is carried up from 12 o'clock to 3 o'clock. The tail should not be curled over the back. The long, smooth tail tapers to a point with a brush of hair, also called the Harrier's flag, which is the part of the dog that is most visible while he is working. In England, the Harrier's tail is referred to as a stern.

There should be moderate angulation of the forequarters, with long shoulders sloping into the muscles of the back, clean at the withers. The shoulders are well clothed with muscle without being excessively heavy or loaded, giving the impression of free, strong action. Elbows are set well away from the ribs, running parallel with the body and not turning outwards. The Harrier should possess good straight legs with plenty of bone running well down to the toes. However they should not be overburdened; inclined to knuckle over very slightly, but not exaggerated in the slightest degree. The front feet are round and catlike, with toes set close together and turning slightly inwards. Note, only the AKC standard allows for a degree of "toeing in." This is strongly discouraged in England, as is any degree of "knuckling over," since both are unsound constructions that would be detrimental to long-term working ability. The pads of the feet are thick, well developed, and strong. The Harrier's feet must be able to carry him all day over every type of terrain.

The angulation of the hindquarters is in balance with the front assembly so that rear drive is in harmony with the front reach. Well-developed muscles that provide strength for long hours of work are important. Endurance is more important than pure speed, and as such, the stifles are only moderately angulated. The rear feet point straight ahead, and are round and catlike with toes set close together with thick, well-developed pads.

The Harrier's coat is short, dense, hard, and glossy. Coat texture on the ears is finer than on the body (velvety). The brush on the underside of the tail is hard and abundant. The Harrier comes in a variety of colors, none of which are regarded as more important than any other. By far the most common color is the tri-color. Tri-colors usually have a black saddle with rich tan points and white trimming. There are also tan-and-whites, red-and-whites, lemon-and-whites, solid whites, black-and-tans, and a rarely seen blue-mottled color. Harriers have a tendency to change the degree of color in their coats over their lifetime.

The Harrier's gait reflects the perfect coordination between the front and rear legs. Reach and drive are consistent with the desired moderate angulation. Coming and going, the dog moves in a straight line, evidencing no sign of "crabbing." A slight "toeing in" of the front feet is acceptable. Clean movement coming and going is important, but not as important as a side gait that is smooth, efficient, and covers ground.

The Harrier's temperament is outgoing and friendly. As Harriers must be able to work in packs with other hounds and amidst many strangers in the field, aggressiveness cannot be tolerated. The Harrier is a happy-go-lucky fellow who loves life and his "pack."

The Harrier's temperament is outgoing and friendly and he is happiest when surrounded by his pack, whether canine or human. These three friends are owned by author Donna Smiley-Auborn.

OFFICIAL STANDARD FOR THE HARRIER

General Appearance—Developed in England to hunt hare in packs, Harriers must have all the attributes of a scenting pack hound. They are very sturdily built with large bone for their size. They must be active, well balanced, full of strength and quality, in all ways appearing able to work tirelessly, no matter the terrain, for long periods. Running gear and scenting ability are particularly important features. The Harrier should, in fact, be a smaller version of the English Foxhound.

Size, Proportion, Substance—***Size***—19 to 21 inches for dogs and bitches, variation of one inch in either direction is acceptable. ***Proportion***–is off-square. The Harrier is slightly longer from point of shoulder to rump than from withers to ground. ***Substance***–Solidly built, full of strength and quality. The breed has as much substance and bone as possible without being heavy or coarse.

Head—The head is in proportion to the overall dog. No part of the head should stand out relative to the other parts. The expression is gentle when relaxed, sensible yet alert when aroused. ***Eyes*** are medium size, set well apart, brown or hazel color in darker dogs, lighter hazel to yellow in lighter dogs, though darker colors are always desired. ***Ears*** are set on low and lie close to the cheeks, rounded at the tips.

The ***skull*** is in proportion to the entire animal, with good length and breadth and a bold forehead. The ***stop*** is moderately defined. The ***muzzle*** from stop to tip of nose is approximately the same length as the skull from stop to occiput. The muzzle is substantial with good depth, and the ***lips*** complete the square,

Opposite: Harriers must give the appearance of activity and strength, capable of working tirelessly for long periods of time. Ch. Seaview Knight of Sunnystone, owned by Kathryn Martel and Betty Burnell.

clean look of the muzzle, without excess skin or flews. A good ***nose*** is essential. It must be wide, with well opened nostrils. Teeth meet in a scissors ***bite*** or they may be level. Overshot or undershot bites faulted to the degree of severity of the misalignment.

Neck, Topline, Body–The ***neck*** is long and strong with no excess skin or throatiness, sweeping smoothly into the muscling of the forequarters. The ***topline*** is level. Back muscular with no dip behind the withers or roach over the loin. ***Body***–Chest deep, extending to the elbows, with well sprung ribs that extend well back, providing plenty of heart and lung room. The ribs should not be so well sprung that they interfere with the free, efficient movement of the front assembly. The loin is short, wide and well muscled.

The ***tail*** is long, set on high and carried up from 12 o'clock to 3 o'clock, depending on attitude. It tapers to a point with a brush of hair. The tail should not be curled over the back.

Forequarters—Moderate angulation, with long shoulders sloping into the muscles of the back, clean at the withers. The shoulders are well clothed with muscle without being excessively heavy or loaded, giving the impression of free, strong action. Elbows are set well away from the ribs, running parallel with the body and not turning outwards. Good straight legs with plenty of bone running well down to the toes, but

The Harrier's head should be in proportion to his body and his ears set low, lying close to cheeks.

not overburdened, inclined to knuckle over very slightly but not exaggerated in the slightest degree. ***Feet*** are round and catlike, with toes set close together turning slightly inwards. The pads are thick, well developed and strong.

Opposite: A beautiful head study of Am. Can. Ch. Kingsbury's Without Reservations, CD, owned by authors Donna Smiley-Auborn and John Auborn.

Hindquarters—Angulation in balance with the front assembly, so that rear drive is in harmony with front reach. Well developed muscles, providing strength for long hours of work, are important. Endurance is more important than pure speed, and as such, the stifles are only moderately angulated. ***Feet*** point straight ahead, are round and catlike with toes set close together, and thick, well developed pads.

Coat—Short, dense, hard and glossy. Coat texture on the ears is finer than on the body. There is a brush of hair on the underside of the tail.

Color—Any color, not regarded as very important.

Gait—Perfect coordination between the front and hind legs. Reach and drive are consistent with the desired moderate angulation. Coming and going, the dog moves in a straight line, evidencing no sign of crabbing. A slight toeing-in of the front feet is acceptable. Clean movement coming and going is important, but not nearly as important as side gait, which is smooth, efficient and ground-covering.

Temperament—Outgoing and friendly, as a working pack breed, Harriers must be able to work in close contact with other hounds. Therefore, aggressiveness towards other dogs cannot be tolerated.

Approved December 13, 1988

Effective February 1, 1989

According to the standard, the Harrier's topline should be level and his back muscular. His tail should be long and set on high, depending on his attitude.

CHARACTERISTICS OF THE HARRIER

As with most dog breeds, when looking at a Harrier as a companion, due consideration must be given to their original purpose. Harriers were developed strictly as an active hunting pack hound and are never seen as pets in England, their native country. This does not mean that they will not make good house pets, but their high activity level and need for firm discipline and leadership must be dealt with. As a pack hound,

This four-month-old red and white puppy demonstrates the exuberance and energy that are key Harrier characteristics.

The Kingsbury Pack displays one of the breed's tendencies–howling. These guys think a group howl is even more fun!

Harriers are more social than most other breeds and do best with other dogs or when people are always present. They are strong willed and independent, but with work can be trained to a high level of obedience. If you ever see a mounted huntsman control a pack of 30-60 hounds on paved roads among traffic, you will know what the dogs are capable of doing.

True hounds, Harriers are energetic, independent, self-willed, and persistent. Harriers were bred to work all day (covering 20–40 miles) out in front of hunters, to think things out for themselves, and to never give up the chase, no matter what. Harriers perform their functions remarkably well; hares and foxes have been known to collapse from sheer exhaustion when pursued by tireless Harriers.

Because of their naturally independent and sometimes stubborn nature, obedience training is strongly recommended for all Harriers. If you are looking for a dog that will be constantly underfoot demanding attention with a tennis ball in their mouth or waiting on your next whim, Harriers are not for you. They love being with you, but are not dependent on you for entertainment, because they will entertain themselves. Care needs to be taken to see that Harriers are not allowed to get into unsupervised mischief!

Harriers are full of energy, but are not hyperactive. They are ideally suited to joining you in athletic

The Harrier's love of the outdoors means that he is always ready to have some fun. These two Harriers enjoy a day at the beach.

activities, such as jogging, bicycling, hiking, horseback riding, etc. It is important to avoid hard pavement and excessive speed, as these can be harmful to your Harrier. In the home, they are generally sensible about their activity level and love to share a lap, wrestle with the kids on the floor, or lie on a rug and chew on toys. However, Harriers are generally not recommended as apartment pets for most people, except for those willing to put forth the extra effort to provide adequate training and lots of daily exercise.

Developed as a working pack hound, Harriers are by nature gregarious, friendly hounds that get along well in large numbers. They should never be aggressive to either people or other dogs. They usually fit in nicely with other pets—dogs, cats, horses, etc. If someone is not at home most of the time with your Harrier, it is recommended that you consider getting another dog as a companion, since most Harriers seem happiest when they have a canine buddy to play with while you are gone for the day. It is not necessary that the other dog is a Harrier, just as long as he has a similar personality and activity level and he isn't too frail or tiny to safely handle rough Harrier playing.

Harriers have a truly outstanding temperament—friendly, outgoing, and fun loving. They have an expansive love of life and a healthy sense of humor. They seem to innately love children; they are sturdy and patient enough to put up with endless play, grasping fingers, and clumsy feet with hardly a complaint. As a rule of common sense, dogs and young children should never be left together unsupervised. Harriers are very affectionate, sweet, and loving hounds that tend to view every stranger as just an old friend that they haven't yet met. As such, Harriers do not make good guard dogs. They are, however, good watchdogs. They will most certainly notice anything unusual and will sound the alarm with a loud, alert voice.

Harriers are generally not recommended for novice or first-time dog owners. The biggest problem seen in raising Harriers is the lack of consistent discipline and leadership. The average person, who would do well with an unchallenging breed such as a Shetland Sheepdog or Golden Retriever, may not be adequately prepared for the needs of a strong-willed, independent Harrier. The majority of Harriers surrendered to HCA Rescue are hounds that have become unmanageable to their family. When retrained in rescue programs, it is abundantly clear that these Harriers had been raised without effective discipline or a clear leader to set firm house rules and enforce them. You *cannot* allow a Harrier to take charge. They need and look for a leader, which is your job and responsibility. This does not mean that you have to be heavy-handed, just that you must set clear rules for acceptable behavior and then follow through to make sure that they are obeyed consistently.

Harriers have truly wonderful, gentle personalities and make loving pets. Author Donna Smiley-Auborn cuddles with her girl Jessie on the couch.

Going to one can be great fun for you and your hound, since they are securely fenced, and as long as your hound is cordial with other dogs, this offers wonderful off-leash play situations with their "doggie friends."

OTHER HARRIER ESSENTIALS

A Securely Fenced Yard

If given the opportunity (such as an open gate or broken fence) most Harriers will not think twice before taking off in pursuit of any interesting scents that they chance upon. While they will usually return home if they are able, a secure yard will prevent them from getting lost, injured, or killed. Underground "fenceless" electronic systems have *not* been 100 percent effective, as many Harriers consider the brief shock from crossing the underground line well worth it if they get to chase or investigate something interesting outside their yard. Additionally, unlike normal fencing, these electronic systems do not prevent stray animals from coming into your yard and causing trouble with your hound, nor do they encourage your hound to return to his own yard if he has escaped, because of his fear of that second shock.

Most Harriers will not think twice about taking off in pursuit of an interesting scent. Therefore, a securely fenced-in yard is a must for all Harrier owners.

Good Nutrition

This means that a high-quality commercial dog food should be used—not table scraps or cheap dog food from the grocery store. Dry food is preferred over canned or semi-moist foods, since the dry food by nature helps to keep the teeth cleaner than wet foods. Canned foods are mostly water, so the nutritional value is much lower. Semi-moist foods, like the kinds that are advertised as "burgers," not only gum up the dog's teeth, but also contain formaldehyde to keep them in their semi-soft state. Why would you want to feed your dog formaldehyde? While cheap dog foods may be attractive because of their low cost, by volume they are made up of mostly filler (i.e., peanut shells and other non-nutritional ingredients) that provides bulk without much nutritional value. This added bulk will also give you a higher volume of waste to pick up in the yard. Go with a premium-type food that has quality meat and grains (i.e., lamb, chicken, rice, corn) as their first several ingredients. Besides seeing a better result in your dog through his healthier coat and skin, you will also see a reduction in stool volume since a much greater percentage of the food is useable and digestible to your dog.

We all like to pamper our dogs. However, treats can be a harmful source of useless calories that lead to weight problems and finicky eating habits. Rather than using commercial dog cookies, which are basically the equivalent of doggie potato chips, try feeding raw fruits and vegetables as treats instead. Most Harriers enjoy whole apples or apple slices, grapes, plums, watermelon, and carrots. Be creative and try whatever fruit or veggies you have on hand (except for onions and green potatoes, which can be poisonous to dogs). These are guilt-free treats that you can feel good about, since they are nutritional as well as tasty.

Treats can be used as motivation when training your Harrier, but make sure the treats are nutritious and do not upset your dog's regular feeding schedule.

CHA

GROOMING YOUR HARRIER

The Harrier is predominantly a wash-and-wear type of dog. There is not much regular grooming necessary to keep your Harrier in good condition.

BASIC GROOMING EQUIPMENT

You will need the following:

Stainless steel, fine-toothed comb;
Bristle brush;
Hound glove or piece of chamois;
Nail clipper (or grinder tool, optional);
Styptic powder;
Cotton balls;
Ear cleaning solution;
Dental kit (toothbrush and toothpaste for dogs);
All-purpose stripping knife (also called a blade or rake);
(Optional) No-rinse shampoo.

Although Harriers do not require daily coat care, they do need regular maintenance to look their healthy best. A once-per-week routine should be enjoyable for both you and your Harrier. Start your routine with a "full body massage," by running your hands over your dog's entire body. Feel for any areas that may be hard or for lumps or bumps that were not there the week before. If you find something that concerns you, call your vet. It is better to be safe than sorry with your companion. After the massage, your dog should be calm and relaxed. This is the perfect time to trim the toenails. Use your toenail clippers judiciously. Take off only the tips using a quick stroke. You can smooth the edges of the trimmed toenail with a metal nail file.

If this is done every week, you will have an easy job. If you make a mistake and take too much off, *do not panic*. Although you will probably hear an earth-shattering scream and see more blood than you can imagine, be calm and follow these steps.

1. Take a deep breath.
2. Keep hold of the dog.
3. Open your styptic powder (*never* clip nails without it handy).
4. Take out a good-sized pinch and apply it directly to the bleeding nail. Don't worry if it takes several applications for the bleeding to stop.
5. Continue breathing and reassure yourself and your dog that you both will indeed survive.
6. Continue trimming the rest of the nails.

An alternative to nail clippers is the use of an electric grinder tool with a sandpaper wheel. This is used to grind down and shape the nail and is less likely to take too much off the nail.

After nail trimming, move to ear care. Apply ear-cleaning solution to the cotton ball. Wipe out any accumulated dirt and residue from the visible ear canal crevices. If there is more dirt or residue that you cannot easily reach, call your vet. Remember to use different cotton balls for each ear.

Although the Harrier is basically a "wash-and-wear" breed, regular grooming will help keep your dog looking his best.

After the ears, move to the coat. Start with a simple

combing over the body to remove any dead hair. Follow up with a once-over with the bristle brush. During shedding season, begin this process by running the stripping knife over the dog's entire coat until you have most of the dead hair out. For "spot cleaning" (when a full bath is not necessary) use a bit of no-rinse shampoo. This watery solution is usually blue in color. Rub it in, then towel dry the area. Finish your coat care with a good once-over with the chamois cloth or hound glove. This will give a remarkable sheen to the coat.

Last, but not least, is dental care. As silly as it may seem, the several minutes that you spend brushing your Harrier's teeth may save you hundreds of dollars in veterinary bills and untold discomfort to your dog.

If you feel that you must trim something on your Harrier with a pair of scissors, you can cut his whiskers for a less "scruffy" appearance and round off the tip of his tail. Bathe your Harrier only as needed so that you do not deplete the coat's natural oils. That is all that is necessary for the proper grooming of a Harrier. A simple weekly routine should run about 15 minutes (25-30 minutes during shedding season).

A thorough oral examination and dental care should be a part of your Harrier's grooming routine.

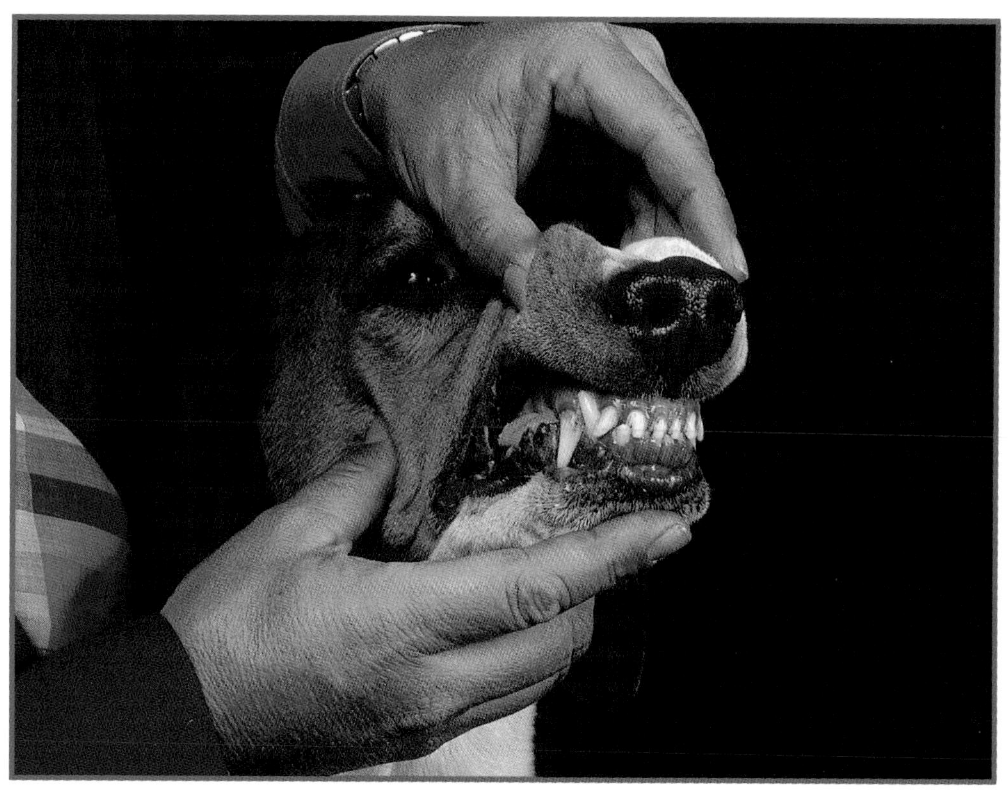

YOUR PUPPY'S NEW HOME

Before actually collecting your puppy, it is better that you purchase the basic items you will need in advance of the pup's arrival date. This allows you more opportunity to shop around and ensure you have exactly what you want rather than having to buy lesser quality in a hurry.

It is always better to collect the puppy as early in the day as possible. In most instances this will mean that the puppy has a few hours with your family before it is time to retire for his first night's sleep away from his former home.

If the breeder is local, then you may not need any form of box to place the puppy in when you bring him home. A member of the family can hold the pup in his lap—duly protected by some towels just in case the puppy becomes car sick! Be sure to advise the breeder at what time you hope to arrive for the puppy, as this will obviously influence the feeding of the pup that morning or afternoon. If you arrive early in the day, then they will likely only give the pup a light breakfast so as to reduce the risk of travel sickness.

If the trip will be of a few hours duration, you should take a travel crate with you. The crate will provide your pup with a safe place to lie down and rest during the trip. During the trip, the puppy will no doubt wish to relieve his bowels, so you will have to make a few stops. On a long journey you may need a rest yourself, and can take the opportunity to let the puppy get some fresh air. However, do not let the puppy walk where there may have been a lot of other dogs because he might pick up an infection. Also, if he relieves his

This is a pup with potential! Eight-week-old Amblin's Kingsbury Armageddon shows correct substance and proportions.

bowels at such a time, do not just leave the feces where they were dropped. This is the height of irresponsibility. It has resulted in many public parks and other places actually banning dogs. You can purchase poop-scoops from your pet shop and should have them with you whenever you are taking the dog out where he might foul a public place.

Your journey home should be made as quickly as possible. If it is a hot day, be sure the car interior is amply supplied with fresh air. It should never be too hot or too cold for the puppy. The pup must never be placed where he might be subject to a draft. If the journey requires an overnight stop at a motel, be aware that other guests will not appreciate a puppy crying half the night. You must regard the puppy as a baby and comfort him so he does not cry for long periods. The worst thing you can do is to shout at or smack him. This will mean your relationship is off to a really bad start. You wouldn't smack a baby, and your puppy is still very much just this.

ON ARRIVING HOME

By the time you arrive home the puppy may be very tired, in which case he should be taken to his sleeping area and allowed to rest. Children should not be allowed to interfere with the pup when he is sleeping. If the pup is not tired, he can be allowed to investigate his new home—but always under your close supervision. After a short look around, the puppy will no doubt appreciate a light meal and a drink of water. Do not overfeed him at his first meal because he will be in an excited state and more likely to be sick.

Although it is an obvious temptation, you should not invite friends and neighbors around to see the new arrival until he has had at least 48 hours in which to settle down. Indeed, if you can delay this longer then do so, especially if the puppy is not fully vaccinated. At the very least, the visitors might introduce some local bacteria on their clothing that the puppy is not immune to. This aspect is always a risk when a pup has been moved some distance, so the fewer people the pup meets in the first week or so the better.

Puppies can be irresistible, but make sure you carefully research the Harrier's needs before deciding to take one home.

DANGERS IN THE HOME

Your home holds many potential dangers for a little mischievous puppy, so you must think about these in advance and be sure he is protected from them. The more obvious are as follows:

Open Fires. All open fires should be protected by a mesh screen guard so there is no danger of the pup being burned by spitting pieces of coal or wood.

Electrical Wires. Puppies just love chewing on things, so be sure that all electrical appliances are neatly hidden from view and are not left plugged in when not in use. It is not sufficient simply to turn the plug switch to the off position—pull the plug from the socket.

Open Doors. A door would seem a pretty innocuous object, yet with a strong draft it could kill or injure a puppy easily if it is slammed shut. Always ensure there is no risk of this happening. It is most likely during warm weather when you have windows or outside doors open and a sudden gust of wind blows through.

Balconies. If you live in a high-rise building, obviously the pup must be protected from falling. Be sure he cannot get through any railings on your patio, balcony, or deck.

Ponds and Pools. A garden pond or a swimming pool is a very dangerous place for a little puppy to be near. Be sure it is well screened so there is no risk of the pup falling in. It takes barely a minute for a pup—or a child—to drown.

The Kitchen. While many puppies will be kept in the kitchen, at least while they are toddlers and not able to control their bowel movements, this is a room full of danger—especially while you are cooking. When cooking, keep the puppy in a play pen or in another room where he is safely out of harm's way. Alternatively, if you have a carry box or crate, put him in this so he can still see you but is well protected.

Be aware, when using washing machines, that

When properly introduced, your Harrier should get along fine with other pets.

Puppies can get into a lot of mischief; so make sure they have a safe place to play when outside and are always closely supervised.

more than one puppy has clambered in and decided to have a nap and received a wash instead! If you leave the washing machine door open and leave the room for any reason, then be sure to check inside the machine before you close the door and switch on.

Small Children. Toddlers and small children should never be left unsupervised with puppies. In spite of such advice it is amazing just how many people not only do this but also allow children to pull and maul pups. They should be taught from the outset that a puppy is not a plaything to be dragged about the home—and they should be promptly scolded if they disobey.

Children must be shown how to lift a puppy so it is safe. Failure by you to correctly educate your children about dogs could one day result in their getting a very nasty bite or scratch. When a puppy is lifted, his weight must always be supported. To lift the pup, first place your right hand under his chest. Next, secure the pup by using your left hand to hold his neck. Now you can lift him and bring him close to your chest. Never lift a pup by his ears and, while he can be lifted by the scruff of his neck where the fur is loose, there is no reason ever to do this, so don't.

Beyond the dangers already cited you may be able to think of other ones that are specific to your home—steep basement steps or the like. Go around your

Harriers get along very well in large groups. Here, four Harriers and a Dalmatian find a warm spot by the fireplace.

and watch them from a suitable vantage point. Eventually they will meet at ground level where the cat will quickly hiss and box a puppy's ears. The pup will soon learn to respect an adult cat; thereafter they will probably develop into great friends as the pup matures into an adult dog.

HOUSETRAINING

Undoubtedly, the first form of training your puppy will undergo is in respect to his toilet habits. To achieve this you can use either newspaper, or a large litter tray filled with soil or lined with newspaper. A puppy cannot control his bowels until he is a few months old, and not fully until he is an adult. Therefore you must anticipate his needs and be prepared for a few accidents. The prime times a pup will urinate and defecate are shortly after he wakes up from a sleep, shortly after he has eaten, and after he has been playing awhile. He will usually whimper and start searching the room for a suitable place. You must quickly pick him up and place him on the newspaper or in the litter tray. Hold him in position gently but firmly. He might jump out of the box without doing anything on the first one or two occasions, but if you simply repeat the procedure every time you think he wants to relieve himself then eventually he will get the message.

When he does defecate as required, give him plenty of praise, telling him what a good puppy he is. The litter tray or newspaper must, of course, be cleaned or replaced after each use—puppies do not like using a dirty toilet any more than you do. The pup's toilet can be placed near the kitchen door and as he gets older the tray can be placed outside while the door is open. The pup will then start to use it while he is outside. From that time on, it is easy to get the pup to use a given area of the yard.

Many breeders recommend the popular alternative of crate training. Upon bringing the pup home, introduce him to his crate. The open wire crate is the best choice, placed in a restricted, draft-free area of the

Harriers have a wonderful sense of humor and an easygoing nature, which makes them great companions for children. Seven-week-old "Music" is the perfect straight man.

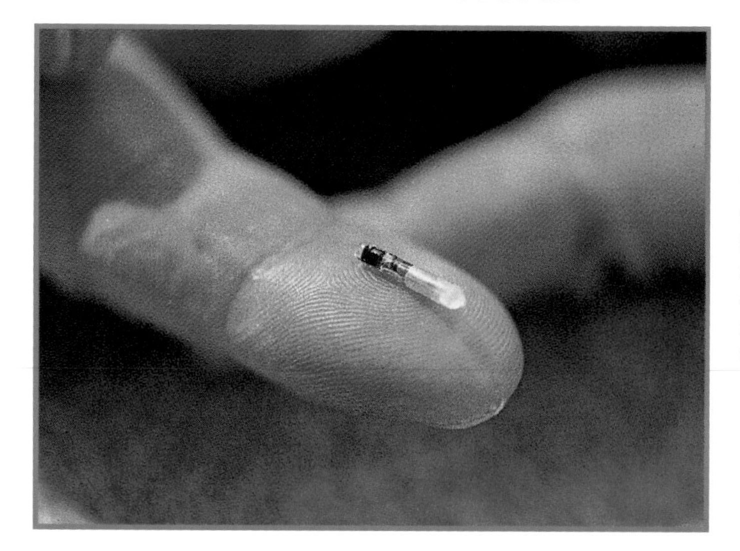

The newest method of identification is the microchip, a computer chip that is no bigger than a grain of rice that is injected into the dog's skin.

clearly someone's pet, and not abandoned animals. As a result, thieves will normally abandon dogs so marked and this at least gives the dog a chance to be taken to the police or the dog pound, when the number can be traced and the dog reunited with his family. The only problem with this method at this time is that there are a number of registration bodies, so it is not always apparent which one the dog is registered with (as you provide the actual number). However, each registration body is aware of his competitors and will normally be happy to supply their addresses. Those holding the dog can check out which one you are with. It is not a perfect system, but until such is developed it's the best available.

Another permanent form of identification is the microchip, a computer chip that is no bigger than a grain of rice that is injected between the dog's shoulder blades. The dog feels no discomfort. The dog also receives a tag that says he is microchipped. If the dog is lost and picked up by the humane society, they can trace the owner by scanning the microchip. It is the safest form of identification.

A temporary tag takes the form of a metal or plastic disk large enough for you to place the dog's name and your phone number on it—maybe even your address as well. In virtually all places you will be required to obtain a license for your puppy. This may not become applicable until the pup is six months old, but it might apply regardless of his age. Much depends upon the state within a country, or the country itself, so check with your veterinarian if the breeder has not already advised you on this.

FEEDING YOUR HARRIER

Dog owners today are fortunate in that they live in an age when considerable cash has been invested in the study of canine nutritional requirements. This means dog food manufacturers are very concerned about ensuring that their foods are of the best quality. The result of all of their studies, apart from the food itself, is that dog owners are bombarded with advertisements telling them why they must purchase a given brand. The number of products available to you is unlimited, so it is hardly surprising to find that dogs in general suffer from obesity and an excess of vitamins, rather than the reverse. Be sure to feed age-appropriate food—puppy food up to one year of age, adult food thereafter. Generally breeders recommend dry food supplemented by canned, if needed.

FACTORS AFFECTING NUTRITIONAL NEEDS

Activity Level. A dog that lives in a country environment and is able to exercise for long periods of the day will need more food than the same breed of dog living in an apartment and given little exercise.

Quality of the Food. Obviously the quality of food

Newborn puppies have all their nutritional needs met through nursing. Once they are weaned it is up to you, the owner to provide a healthy diet.

will affect the quantity required by a puppy. If the nutritional content of a food is low then the puppy will need more of it than if a better quality food was fed.

Balance of Nutrients and Vitamins. Feeding a puppy the correct balance of nutrients is not easy because the average person is not able to measure out ratios of one to another, so it is a case of trying to see that nothing is in excess. However, only tests, or your veterinarian, can be the source of reliable advice.

Genetic and Biological Variation. Apart from all of the other considerations, it should be remembered that each puppy is an individual. His genetic make-up will influence not only his physical characteristics but also his metabolic efficiency. This being so, two pups from the same litter can vary quite a bit in the amount of food they need to perform the same function under the same conditions. If you consider the potential combinations of all of these factors then you will see that pups of a given breed could vary quite a bit in the amount of food they will need. Before discussing feeding quantities it is valuable to know at least a little about the composition of food and its role in the body.

COMPOSITION AND ROLE OF FOOD

The main ingredients of food are protein, fats, and carbohydrates, each of which is needed in relatively large quantities when compared to the other needs of vitamins and minerals. The other vital ingredient of food is, of course, water. Although all foods obviously contain some of the basic ingredients needed for an animal to survive, they do not all contain the ingredients in the needed ratios or type. For example, there are many forms of protein, just as there are many types of carbohydrates. Both of these compounds are found in meat and in vegetable matter—but not all of those that are needed will be in one particular meat or vegetable. Plants, especially, do not contain certain amino acids that are required for the synthesis of certain proteins needed by dogs.

Likewise, vitamins are found in meats and vegetable matter, but vegetables are a richer source of most. Meat contains very little carbohydrates. Some vitamins can be synthesized by the dog, so do not need to be supplied via the food. Dogs are carnivores and this means their digestive tract has evolved to need a high quantity of meat as compared to humans. The digestive system of carnivores is unable to break down the tough cellulose walls of plant matter, but it

is easily able to assimilate proteins from meat.

In order to gain its needed vegetable matter in a form that it can cope with, the carnivore eats all of its prey. This includes the partly digested food within the stomach. In commercially prepared foods, the cellulose is broken down by cooking. During this process the vitamin content is either greatly reduced or lost altogether. The manufacturer therefore adds vitamins once the heat process has been completed. This is why commercial foods are so useful as part of a feeding regimen, providing they are of good quality and from a company that has prepared the foods very carefully.

Proteins

These are made from amino acids, of which at least ten are essential if a puppy is to maintain healthy growth. Proteins provide the building blocks for the puppy's body. The richest sources are meat, fish and poultry, together with their by-products. The latter will include milk, cheese, yogurt, fishmeal, and eggs. Vegetable matter that has a high protein content includes soy beans, together with numerous corn and other plant extracts that have been dehydrated. The actual protein content needed in the diet will be determined both by the activity level of the dog and his age. The total protein need will also be influenced by the digestibility factor of the food given.

Fats

These serve numerous roles in the puppy's body.

POPpups™ are 100% edible and enhanced with dog-friendly ingredients like liver, cheese, spinach, chicken, carrots, or potatoes. They contain no salt, sugar, alcohol, plastic or preservatives. You can even microwave a POPpup™ to turn into a huge crackly treat.

They provide insulation against the cold, and help buffer the organs from knocks and general activity shocks. They provide the richest source of energy, and reserves of this, and they are vital in the transport of vitamins and other nutrients, via the blood, to all other organs. Finally, it is the fat content within a diet that gives it palatability. It is important that the fat content of a diet should not be excessive. This is because the high energy content of fats (more than twice that of protein or carbohydrates) will increase the overall energy content of the diet. The puppy will adjust his food intake to that of his energy needs, which are obviously more easily met in a high-energy diet. This will mean that while the fats are providing the energy needs of the puppy, the overall diet may not be providing his protein, vitamin, and mineral needs, so signs of protein deficiency will become apparent. Rich sources of fats are meat, their byproducts (butter, milk), and vegetable oils, such as safflower, olive, corn or soy bean.

Carbohydrates

These are the principal energy compounds given to puppies and adult dogs. Their inclusion within most commercial brand dog foods is for cost, rather than dietary needs. These compounds are more commonly known as sugars, and they are seen in simple or complex compounds of carbon, hydrogen, and oxygen. One of the simple sugars is called glucose, and it is vital to many metabolic processes. When large chains of glucose are created, they form compound sugars. One of these is called glycogen, and it is found in the cells of animals. Another, called starch,

You must choose a dog food for your Harrier based on his age and activity level. Harriers that work outdoors, like Dixie, will need a high-energy diet.

Carrots are rich in fiber, carbohydrates, and vitamin A. The Carrot Bone™ by Nylabone® is a durable chew containing no plastics or artificial ingredients and it can be served as-is, in a bone-hard form, or microwaved to a biscuit consistency.

is the material that is found in the cells of plants.

Vitamins

These are not foods as such but chemical compounds that assist in all aspects of an animal's life. They help in so many ways that to attempt to describe these effectively would require a chapter in itself. Fruits are a rich source of vitamins, as is the liver of most animals. Many vitamins are unstable and easily destroyed by light, heat, moisture, or rancidity. An excess of vitamins, especially A and D, has been proven to be very harmful. Provided a puppy is receiving a balanced diet, it is most unlikely there will be a deficiency, whereas hypervitaminosis (an excess of vitamins) has become quite common due to owners and breeders feeding unneeded supplements. The only time you should feed extra vitamins to your puppy is if your veterinarian advises you to.

Minerals

These provide strength to bone and cell tissue, as well as assist in many metabolic processes. Examples are calcium, phosphorous, copper, iron, magnesium, selenium, potassium, zinc, and sodium. The recommended amounts of all minerals in the diet has not been fully established. Calcium and phosphorous are known to be important, especially to puppies. They help in forming strong bone. As with vitamins, a mineral deficiency is most unlikely in pups given a good and varied diet. Again, an excess can create problems—this applying equally to calcium.

Water

This is the most important of all nutrients, as is easily shown by the fact that the adult dog is made up of about 60 percent water, the puppy containing an even higher percentage. Dogs must retain a water balance, which means that the total intake should be balanced by the total output. The intake comes either by direct input (the tap or its equivalent), plus water released when food is oxidized, known as metabolic water (remember that all foods contain the elements hydrogen and oxygen that recombine in the body to create water). A dog without adequate water will lose condition more rapidly than one depleted of food, a fact common to most animal species.

AMOUNT TO FEED

The best way to determine dietary requirements is by observing the puppy's general health and physical appearance. If he is well covered with flesh, shows good bone development and muscle, and is an active alert puppy, then his diet is fine. A puppy will consume about twice as much as an adult (of the same breed). You should ask the breeder of your puppy to show you the amounts fed to their pups and this will be a good starting point.

The puppy should eat his meal in about five to seven minutes. Any leftover food can be discarded or

Make sure you always have clean, cool water available to your Harrier at all times. This pup thinks one sip is just not enough!

A nutritious diet will be evident in your Harrier's shiny coat, bright eyes, and overall healthy appearance.

placed into the refrigerator until the next meal (but be sure it is thawed fully if your fridge is very cold).

If the puppy quickly devours his meal and is clearly still hungry, then you are not giving him enough food. If he eats readily but then begins to pick at it, or walks away leaving a quantity, then you are probably giving him too much food. Adjust this at the next meal and you will quickly begin to appreciate what the correct amount is. If, over a number of weeks, the pup starts to look fat, then he is obviously overeating; the reverse is true if he starts to look thin compared with others of the same breed.

WHEN TO FEED

It really does not matter what times of the day the puppy is fed, as long as he receives the needed quantity of food. Puppies from 8 weeks to 12 or 16 weeks need 3 or 4 meals a day. Older puppies and adult dogs should be fed twice a day. What is most important is that the feeding times are reasonably regular. They can be tailored to fit in with your own timetable—for example, 7 a.m. and 6 p.m. The dog will then expect his meals at these times each day. Keeping regular feeding times and feeding set amounts will help you monitor your puppy's or dog's health. If a dog that's normally enthusiastic about mealtimes and eats readily suddenly shows a lack of interest in food, you'll know something's not right.

TRAINING YOUR HARRIER

Once your puppy has settled into your home and responds to his name, then you can begin his basic training. Before giving advice on how you should go about doing this, two important points should be made. You should train the puppy in isolation of any potential distractions, and you should keep all lessons very short. It is essential that you have the full attention of your puppy. This is not possible if there are other people about, or televisions and radios on, or other pets in the vicinity. Even when the pup has become a young adult, the maximum time you should allocate to a lesson is about 20 minutes. However, you can give the puppy more than one lesson a day, three being as many as are recommended, each well spaced apart.

Before beginning a lesson, always play a little game with the puppy so he is in an active state of mind and thus more receptive to the matter at hand. Likewise, always end a lesson with fun-time for the pup, and always—this is most important—end on a high note, praising the puppy. Let the lesson end when the pup has done as you require so he receives lots of fuss. This will really build his confidence.

COLLAR AND LEASH TRAINING

Training a puppy to his collar and leash is very easy. Place a collar on the puppy and, although he will initially try to bite at it, he will soon forget it, the more so if you play with him. You can leave the collar on for a few hours. Some people leave their dogs' collars on all of the time, others only when they are taking the dog out. If it is to be left on, purchase a narrow or round one so it does not mark the fur.

Once the puppy ignores his collar, then you can attach the leash to it and let the puppy pull this along behind him for a few minutes. However, if the pup

From the very beginning of your relationship, you must establish household rules for your Harrier. This eight-week-old pup was caught red-handed!

starts to chew at the leash, simply hold the leash but keep it slack and let the pup go where he wants. The idea is to let him get the feel of the leash, but not get in the habit of chewing it. Repeat this a couple of times a day for two days and the pup will get used to the leash without thinking that it will restrain him—which you will not have attempted to do yet.

Next, you can let the pup understand that the leash will restrict his movements. The first time he realizes this, he will pull and buck or just sit down. Immediately call the pup to you and give him lots of fuss. Never tug on the leash so the puppy is dragged along the floor, as this simply implants a negative thought in his mind.

THE COME COMMAND

Come is the most vital of all commands and especially so for the independently minded dog. To teach the puppy to come, let him reach the end of a long lead, then give the command and his name, gently pulling him toward you at the same time. As soon as he associates the word come with the action of moving toward you, pull only when he does not

These two Harriers enjoy the show life, although the one on the bottom wishes her sister would find another place to "sit."

one is attempted. This is so the puppy always starts, as well as ends, a lesson on a high note, having successfully completed something.

Call the puppy to you and fuss over him. Place one hand on his hindquarters and the other under his upper chest. Say "Sit" in a pleasant (never harsh) voice. At the same time, push down his rear end and push up under his chest. Now lavish praise on the puppy. Repeat this a few times and your pet will get the idea. Once the puppy is in the sit position you will release your hands. At first he will tend to get up, so immediately repeat the exercise. The lesson will end when the pup is in the sit position. When the puppy understands the command, and does it right away, you can slowly move backwards so that you are a few feet away from him. If he attempts to come to you, simply place him back in the original position and start again. Do not attempt to keep the pup in the sit position for too long. At this age, even a few seconds is a long while and you do not want him to get bored with lessons before he has even begun them.

THE HEEL COMMAND

All dogs should be able to walk nicely on a leash without their owners being involved in a tug-of-war. The heel command will follow leash training. Heel training is best done where you have a wall to one side of you. This will restrict the puppy's lateral movements, so you only have to contend with forward and backward situations. A fence is an alternative, or you can do the lesson in the garage. Again, it is better to do the lesson in private, not on a public sidewalk where there will be many distractions.

With a puppy, there will be no need to use a choke collar as you can be just as effective with a regular one. The leash should be of good length, certainly not too short. You can adjust the space between you, the puppy, and the wall so your pet has only a small amount of room to move sideways. This being so, he will either hang back or pull ahead—the latter is the more desirable state as it indicates a bold pup who is not frightened of you.

Hold the leash in your right hand and pass it through your left. As the puppy moves ahead and strains on the leash, give the leash a quick jerk backwards with

The versatile Harrier can accomplish almost anything. Wesford's Morning Thunder quickly catches the scent in a tracking trial.

The graceful and swift-moving Harrier is a natural to compete in many events–including agility. Ranger, owned by Betty Burnell, sails through the tire jump effortlessly.

your left hand, at the same time saying "Heel." The position you want the pup to be in is such that his chest is level with, or just behind, an imaginary line from your knee. When the puppy is in this position, praise him and begin walking again, and the whole exercise will be repeated. Once the puppy begins to get the message, you can use your left hand to pat the side of your knee so the pup is encouraged to keep close to your side.

It is useful to suddenly do an about-turn when the pup understands the basics. The puppy will now be behind you, so you can pat your knee and say "Heel." As soon as the pup is in the correct position, give him lots of praise. The puppy will now be beginning to associate certain words with certain actions. Whenever he is not in the heel position he will experience displeasure as you jerk the leash, but when he comes alongside you he will receive praise. Given these two options, he will always prefer the latter—assuming he has no other reason to fear you, which would then create a dilemma in his mind.

Once the lesson has been well learned, then you

can adjust your pace from a slow walk to a quick one and the puppy will come to adjust. The slow walk is always the more difficult for most puppies, as they are usually anxious to be on the move.

If you have no wall to walk against then things will be a little more difficult because the pup will tend to wander to his left. This means you need to give lateral jerks as well as bring the pup to your side. End the lesson when the pup is walking nicely beside you. Begin the lesson with a few sit commands (which he understands by now), so you're starting with success and praise. If your puppy is nervous on the leash, you should never drag him to your side as you may see so many other people do (who obviously didn't invest in a good book like you did!). If the pup sits down, call him to your side and give lots of praise. The pup must always come to you because he wants to. If he is dragged to your side he will see you doing the dragging—a big negative. When he races ahead he does not see you jerk the leash, so all he knows is that something restricted his movement and, once he was in a given position, you gave him lots of praise. This is using canine psychology to your advantage.

With the proper training, the Harrier can make a well-mannered companion and housedog. These four perform the stay command while posing for a family photo.

Always try to remember that if a dog must be disciplined, then try not to let him associate the discipline with you. This is not possible in all matters but, where it is, this is definitely to be preferred.

THE STAY COMMAND

This command follows from the sit. Face the puppy and say "Sit." Now step backwards, and as you do, say "Stay." Let the pup remain in the position for only a few seconds before calling him to you and giving lots of praise. Repeat this, but step further back. You do not need to shout at the puppy. Your pet is not deaf; in fact, his hearing is far better than yours. Speak just loudly enough for the pup to hear, yet use a firm voice. You can stretch the word to form a "sta-a-a-y." If the pup gets up and comes to you simply lift him up, place him back in the original position, and start again. As the pup comes to understand the command, you can move further and further back.

The next test is to walk away after placing the pup. This will mean your back is to him, which will tempt him to follow you. Keep an eye over your shoulder, and the minute the pup starts to move, spin around and, using a sterner voice, say either "Sit" or "Stay." If the pup has gotten quite close to you, then, again, return him to the original position.

As the weeks go by you can increase the length of time the pup is left in the stay position—but two to

Am. Int. Mex. Ch. Seaview Sun Runner, CD, NA, CGC, or "Ranger," owned by Betty Burnell, is not only a well-rounded champion, he is also a registered therapy dog.

Sunnystone Patriot, owned by Kathryn Martel and Luci Zahray, clears a jump in a UKC agility trial with ease.

three minutes is quite long enough for a puppy. If your puppy drops into a lying position and is clearly more comfortable, there is nothing wrong with this. Likewise, your pup will want to face the direction in which you walked off. Some trainers will insist that the dog faces the direction he was placed in, regardless of whether you move off on his blind side. I have never believed in this sort of obedience because it has no practical benefit.

THE DOWN COMMAND

From the puppy's viewpoint, the down command can be one of the more difficult ones to accept. This is because the position is one taken up by a submissive dog in a wild pack situation. A timid dog will roll over—a natural gesture of submission. A bolder pup will want to get up, and might back off, not feeling he should have to submit to this command. He will feel that he is under attack from you and about to be punished—which is what would be the position in his natural environment. Once he comes to understand this is not the case, he will accept this unnatural position without any problem.

You may notice that some dogs will sit very quickly,

but will respond to the down command more slowly—it is their way of saying that they will obey the command, but under protest!

There are two ways to teach this command. One is, in my mind, more intimidating than the other, but it is up to you to decide which one works best for you. The first method is to stand in front of your puppy and bring him to the sit position, with his collar and leash on. Pass the leash under your left foot so that when you pull on it, the result is that the pup's neck is forced downwards. With your free left hand, push the pup's shoulders down while at the same time saying "Down." This is when a bold pup will instantly try to back off and wriggle in full protest. Hold the pup firmly by the shoulders so he stays in the position for a second or two, then tell him what a good dog he is and give him lots of praise. Repeat this only a few times in a lesson because otherwise the puppy will get bored and upset over this command. End with an easy command that brings back the pup's confidence.

The second method, and the one I prefer, is done as follows: Stand in front of the pup and then tell him to sit. Now kneel down, which is immediately far less intimidating to the puppy than to have you towering above him. Take each of his front legs and pull them forward, at the same time saying "Down." Release the legs and quickly apply light pressure on the shoulders with your left hand. Then, as quickly, say "Good boy" and give lots of fuss. Repeat two or three times only. The pup will learn over a few lessons. Remember, this is a very submissive act on the pup's behalf, so there is no need to rush matters.

RECALL TO HEEL COMMAND

When your puppy is coming to the heel position from an off-leash situation—such as if he has been running free—he should do this in the correct manner. He should pass behind you and take up his position and then sit. To teach this command, have the pup in front of you in the sit position with his collar and leash on. Hold the leash in your right hand. Give him the command to heel, and pat your left knee. As the pup starts to move forward, use your right hand to guide him behind you. If need be you can hold his collar and walk the dog around the back of you to the desired position. You will need to repeat this a few times until the dog understands what is wanted.

When he has done this a number of times, you can try it without the collar and leash. If the pup comes up toward your left side, then bring him to the sit position in front of you, hold his collar and walk him around the back of you. He will eventually understand and automatically pass around your back each time. If the dog is already behind you when you recall him, then he should automatically come to your left side, which you will be patting with your hand.

THE NO COMMAND

This is a command that must be obeyed every time without fail. There are no halfway stages, he must be 100-percent reliable. Most delinquent dogs have never been taught this command; included in these are the jumpers, the barkers, and the biters. Were your puppy to approach a poisonous snake or any other potential danger, the no command, coupled with the recall, could save his life. You do not need to give a specific lesson for this command because it will crop up time and again in day-to-day life.

If the puppy is chewing a slipper, you should approach the pup, take hold of the slipper, and say "No" in a stern voice. If he jumps onto the furniture, lift him off and say "No" and place him gently on the floor. You must be consistent in the use of the command and apply it every time he is doing something you do not want him to do.

Showing off her natural athleticism, Ch. Hartshire's Indoor Fireworks, CD nicely performs the retrieve over the high jump in Open Obedience.

HEALTH CONCERNS OF THE HARRIER

For many years, it was a widely held belief that Harriers were free from genetic problems, mainly due to their obscurity and lack of overbreeding. To a large extent, this opinion has been proven to be true, with one notable exception—hip dysplasia.

Canine Hip Dysplasia (CHD) is an abnormal development of the hip joint where there is a poor fit between the femoral head and the hip socket. Hounds afflicted with CHD can exhibit symptoms that range from very mild (possibly even asymptotic) to severely crippled. Accurate diagnosis is via radiographic X-rays and assessment of the hip joints.

The Orthopedic Foundation for Animals (OFA) is a non-profit organization that evaluates hip X-rays using a panel of veterinary radiologists trained in screening and diagnosing CHD. The X-rays are graded into one of six categories. The three that are certifiably clear of CHD are fair, good, and excellent. The three that exhibit signs of CHD are mild, moderate, and severe. Only those dogs that are clear of CHD after 24 months of age are given an OFA certification number. The current rate of CHD incidence in Harriers is approximately 12 to 15 percent.

The method of inheriting CHD is polygenic, meaning that there are many genes involved, not just a simple single recessive gene. Therefore, it is difficult to pinpoint its exact method of inheritance or to predict exactly what hounds will be affected. However, as the OFA clearly points out, the best method for reducing the incidence of CHD within a breed is by breeding only OFA-clear dogs to OFA-clear dogs (and prefer-

Responsible breeders will only breed quality dogs that have been certified free of genetic defects in order to produce the best puppies possible.

ably breeding only dogs that also have a family history free from CHD). For more information on CHD and OFA, visit their website at http://www.offa.org.

As a responsible puppy buyer, you should only buy from ethical breeders that are concerned about the health and welfare of the breed—ones that can provide you with copies of OFA clearances on both the sire and the dam of the litter in which you are interested. While this will not guarantee that your pup will never develop CHD (since clear parents can produce affected offspring) it will increase your odds considerably.

While genetics plays a large part in CHD, there is also an environmental aspect to the expression of the disorder. If a hound has the genes for bad hips, proper nutrition and exercise will help to decrease or even delay the symptoms. Keep your hound thin and trim, since the excess weight places unwanted stress on the joints. Harriers should not be on puppy formula dog food after six months of age because these formulas contain higher protein and fat ratios that are normally required past that age. There is also some evidence that too much protein and fat in the diet, besides contributing to a weight problem, can also adversely affect joint growth.

The eyes of your Harrier should be clear and free of any redness. Report any signs of irritation directly to your veterinarian.

Avoid hard or stressful exercise (i.e., jogging, biking, excessive jumping) with pups under one year old, since this can also have a negative impact on growing joints. Instead, keep your pup in good physical condition through moderate exercise such as playing in the yard or at the park, and daily walks that increase in length as the pup grows.

EYES

While there has been little incidence of eye problems in Harriers, it is still very important that breeders carefully screen all their hounds for signs of heritable eye disease before breeding. With a gene pool as small as Harriers, no problems can be left to chance, especially when there are reliable screening methods available.

The Canine Eye Registration Foundation (CERF)

is similar to OFA in that it is a non-profit group dedicated to eliminating genetic eye disease in purebred dogs via a national registry. CERF will register dogs as clear of heritable eye disease if they have been examined by a Diplomat of the American College of Veterinary Ophthalmologists (ACVO) and determined to be free of eye abnormalities. Because most eye diseases are progressive in nature, certification is only valid for one year; hounds must be reevaluated annually to stay current with CERF. As with CHD, you should only buy from a breeder that can provide you with current CERF information on both the sire and dam of their litter.

OTHER BREED CONCERNS

In the past, epilepsy was seen on rare occasions in Harriers. Since the problem is much more prevalent in their close cousin, the Beagle, this was not surprising. At the present time, however, thanks to diligent and conscientious breeding practices, epilepsy seems to have been eliminated from the breed.

As has been discussed previously, ideal Harrier temperament should be outgoing, gregarious, friendly, and fun loving. However, temperament problems are known to occur in the breed. The main fault seems to be excessive shyness or skittishness. While most hounds may occasionally react fearfully to a strange situation or a particular person, they should get over it rather quickly and move on. A Harrier with a temperament problem, however, reacts this way to most novel situations and strangers, but without ever getting past their fear. This problem occurs most commonly in pups that are not properly socialized from a young age and exposed adequately to a wide variety of sights, sounds, and situations. Good breeders make every effort to acclimate young pups to strange and potentially frightening sounds—banging pans, screaming children, startling situations, and any other circumstance that might induce timidity or panic in a hound that has been sheltered from such normal daily family activities. A properly bred, raised, and trained Harrier is an ideal companion.

The need for absence of aggression in this breed cannot be stated strongly enough. A Harrier that is aggressive toward either humans or animals is aberrant—period. Such an animal should *never* be used for breeding or represented to the public as a proper example of the breed.

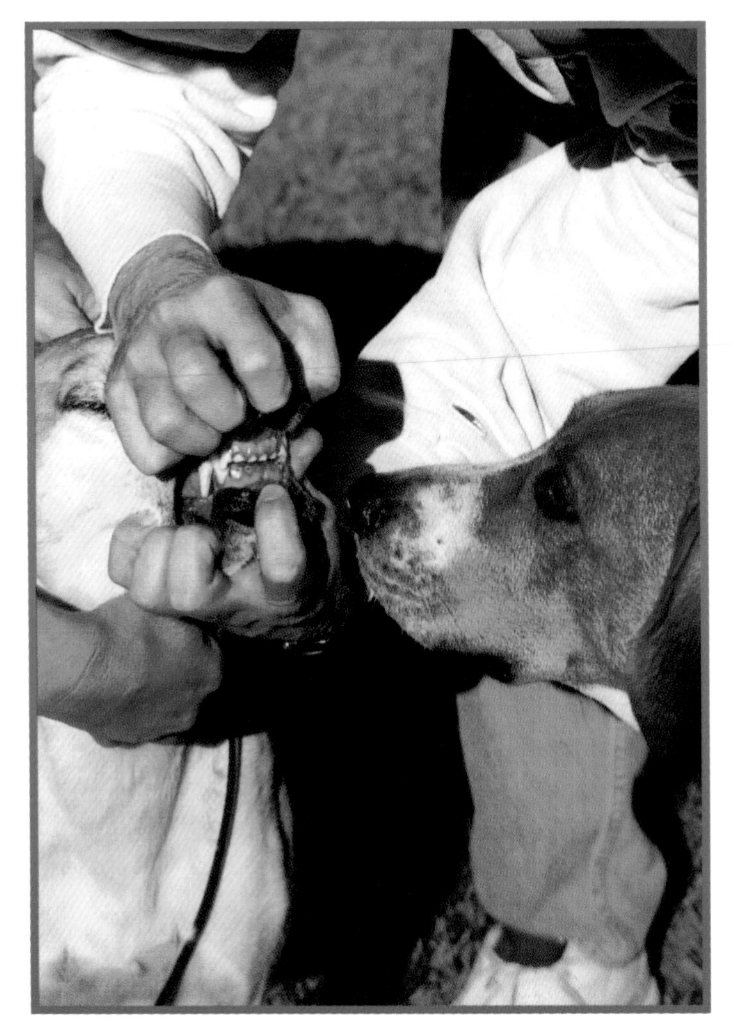

Good preventive dental care will help affect the overall health of your Harrier. This dog's teeth are worn down due to eating raw meat off the bone in English packs for many years.

HEALTHY TEETH AND GUMS

Chewing is instinctual. Puppies chew so that their teeth and jaws grow strong and healthy as they develop. As the permanent teeth begin to emerge, it is painful and annoying to the puppy, and puppy owners must recognize that their new charges need something safe upon which to chew. Unfortunately, once the puppy's permanent teeth have emerged and settled solidly into the jaw, the chewing instinct does not fade. Adult dogs instinctively need to clean their teeth, massage their gums, and exercise their jaws through chewing.

It is necessary for your dog to have clean teeth. You should take your dog to the veterinarian at least once a year to have his teeth cleaned and to have his mouth examined for any sign of oral disease. Although dogs do not get cavities in the same way humans do, dogs'

The Hercules® by Nylabone® has raised dental tips that help fight plaque on your Harrier's teeth and gums.

teeth accumulate tartar, and more quickly than humans do! Veterinarians recommend brushing your dog's teeth daily. But who can find time to brush their dog's teeth daily? The accumulation of tartar and plaque on our dog's teeth when not removed can cause irritation and eventually erode the enamel and finally destroy the teeth. Advanced cases, while destroying the teeth, bring on gingivitis and periodontitis, two very serious conditions that can affect the dog's internal organs as well...to say nothing about bad breath!

Since everyone can't brush their dog's teeth daily or get to the veterinarian often enough for him to scale

Raised dental tips on the surface of every Plaque Attacker™ help to combat plaque and tartar.

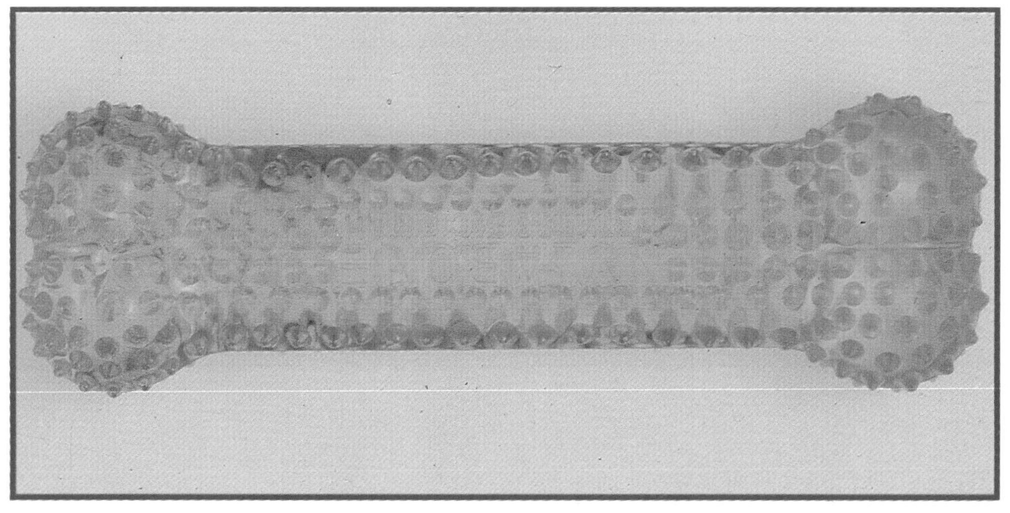

the dog's teeth, providing the dog with something safe to chew on will help maintain oral hygeine. Chew devices from Nylabone® keep dogs' teeth clean, but they also provide an excellent resource for entertainment and relief of doggie tensions. Nylabone® products give your dog something to do for an hour or two every day and during that hour or two, your dog will be taking an active part in keeping his teeth and gums healthy...without even realizing it! That's invaluable to your dog, and valuable to you!

Nylabone® provides fun bones, challenging bones, and *safe* bones. It is an owner's responsibility to recognize safe chew toys from dangerous ones. Your dog will chew and devour anything you give him. Dogs must not be permitted to chew on items that they can break. Pieces of broken objects can do internal damage to a dog, besides ripping the dog's mouth. Cheap plastic or rubber toys can cause stoppage in the intestines; such stoppages are operable only if caught immediately.

The most obvious choices, in this case, may be the worst choice. Natural beef bones were not designed for chewing and cannot take too much pressure from the sides. Due to the abrasive nature of these bones, they should be offered most sparingly. Knuckle bones, though once very popular for dogs, can be easily

Nylabone® is the only plastic dog bone made of 100% virgin nylon, specially processed to create a tough, durable, completely safe bone.

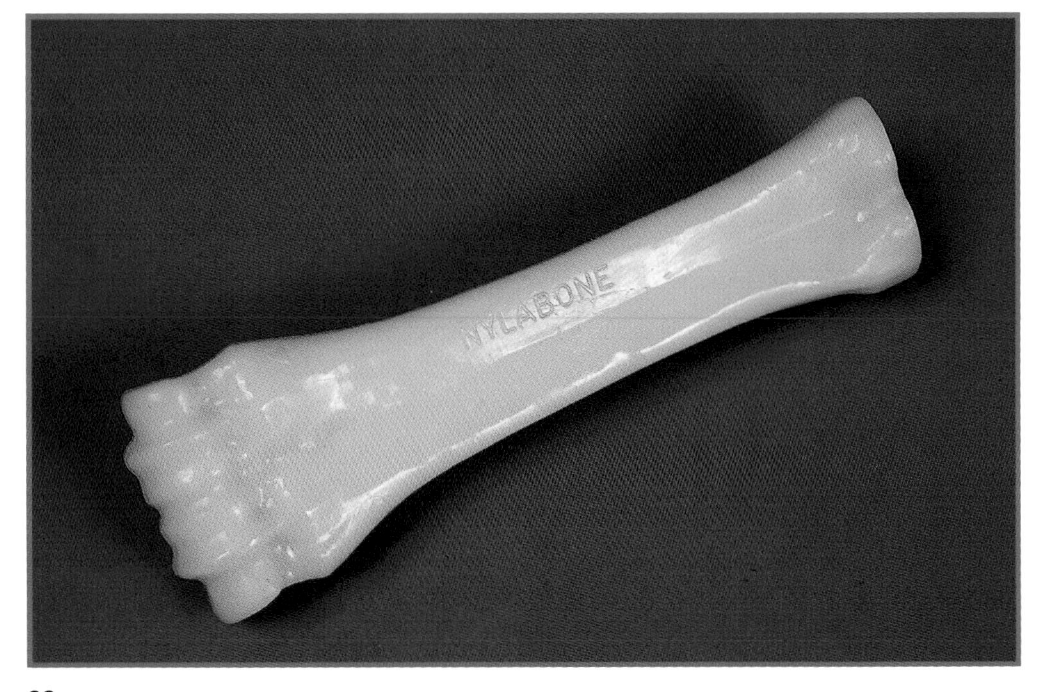

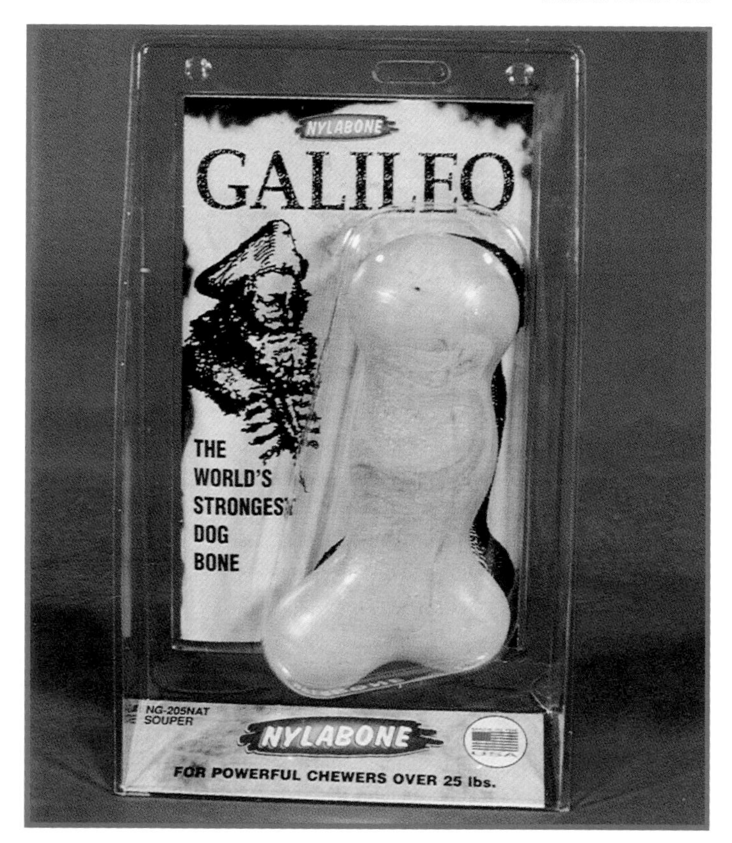

The Galileo™ is flavored to appeal to your dog and annealed so it has a relatively soft outer layer.

chewed up and eaten by dogs. At the very least, digestion is interrupted; at worst, the dog can choke or suffer from intestinal blockage.

When a dog chews hard on a Nylabone®, little bristle-like projections appear on the surface of the bone. These help to clean the dog's teeth and add to the gum-massaging. Given the chemistry of the nylon, the bristle can pass through the dog's intestinal tract without effect. Since nylon is inert, no microorganism can grow on it, and it can be washed in soap and water or sterilized in boiling water or in an autoclave.

For the sake of your dog, his teeth and your own peace of mind, provide your dog with Nylabones®. They have 100 variations from which to choose.

FIGHTING FLEAS

Fleas are very mobile and may be red, black, or brown in color. The adults suck the blood of the host, while the larvae feed on the feces of the adults, which is rich in blood. Flea "dirt" may be seen on the pup as very tiny clusters of blackish specks that look like freshly ground pepper. The eggs of fleas may be laid on the puppy, though they are more commonly laid off the host in a favorable place, such as the bedding. They normally hatch in 4 to 21 days, depending on the temperature, but they can survive for up to 18 months if temperature conditions are not favorable. The larvae are maggot-like and molt a couple of times before forming pupae, which can survive long periods until the temperature, or the vibration of a nearby host, causes them to emerge and jump on a host.

There are a number of effective treatments available, and you should discuss them with your veterinarian, then follow all instructions for the one you choose. Any treatment will involve a product for your puppy or dog and one for the environment, and will require diligence on your part to treat all areas and thoroughly clean your home and yard until the infestation is eradicated.

THE TROUBLE WITH TICKS

Ticks are arthropods of the spider family, which means they have eight legs (though the larvae have six). They bury their headparts into the host and gorge on its blood. They are easily seen as small grain-like creatures sticking out from the skin. They are often picked up when dogs play in fields, but may also arrive in your yard via wild animals—even birds—or stray cats and dogs. Some ticks are species-specific, others are more adaptable and will host on many species.

The cat flea is the most common flea of dogs. It starts feeding soon after it makes contact with the dog.

The deer tick is the most common carrier of Lyme disease. Photo courtesy of Virbac Laboratories, Inc., Fort Worth, Texas.

The most troublesome type of tick is the deer tick, which spreads the deadly Lyme disease that can cripple a dog (or a person). Deer ticks are tiny and very hard to detect. Often, by the time they're big enough to notice, they've been feeding on the dog for a few days—long enough to do their damage. Lyme disease was named for the area of the United States in which it was first detected—Lyme, Connecticut—but has now been diagnosed in almost all parts of the US. Your veterinarian can advise you of the danger to your dog(s) in your area, and may suggest your dog be vaccinated for Lyme. Always go over your dog with a fine-toothed flea comb when you come in from walking through any area that may harbor deer ticks, and if your dog is acting unusually sluggish or sore, seek veterinary advice.

Attempts to pull a tick free will invariably leave the headpart in the pup, where it will die and cause an infected wound or abscess. The best way to remove ticks is to dab a strong saline solution, iodine, or alcohol on them. This will numb them, causing them to loosen their hold, at which time they can be removed with forceps. The wound can then be cleaned and covered with an antiseptic ointment. If ticks are common in your area, consult with your vet for a suitable pesticide to be used in kennels, on bedding, and on the puppy or dog.

INSECTS AND OTHER OUTDOOR DANGERS

There are many biting insects, such as mosquitoes, that can cause discomfort to a puppy. Many attacking bacteria. However, they must first recognize a potential enemy.

Vaccines are either dead bacteria or they are live, but in very small doses. Either type prompts the pup's defense system to attack them. When a large attack then comes (if it does), the immune system recognizes it and massive numbers of lymphocytes (white blood corpuscles) are mobilized to counter the attack. However, the ability of the cells to recognize these dangerous viruses can diminish over a period of time. It is therefore useful to provide annual reminders about the nature of the enemy. This is done by means of booster injections that keep the immune system on its alert. Immunization is not 100-percent guaranteed to be successful, but is very close. Certainly it is better than giving the puppy no protection.

Dogs are subject to other viral attacks, and if these are of a high-risk factor in your area, then your vet will suggest you have the puppy vaccinated against these as well.

Your puppy or dog should also be vaccinated against the deadly rabies virus. In fact, in many places it is illegal for your dog not to be vaccinated. This is to protect your dog, your family, and the rest of the animal population from this deadly virus that infects the nervous system and causes dementia and death.

ACCIDENTS

All puppies will get their share of bumps and bruises due to the rather energetic way they play. These will usually heal themselves over a few days. Small cuts should be bathed with a suitable disinfectant and then smeared with an antiseptic ointment. If a cut looks more serious, then stem the flow of blood with a towel or makeshift tourniquet and rush the pup to the veterinarian. Never apply so much pressure to the wound that it might restrict the flow of blood to the limb.

In the case of burns you should apply cold water or an ice pack to the surface. If the burn was due to a chemical, then this must be washed away with copious amounts of water. Apply petroleum jelly, or any vegetable oil, to the burn. Trim away the hair if need be. Wrap the dog in a blanket and rush him to the vet. The pup may go into shock, depending on the severity of the burn, and this will result in a lowered blood pressure, which is dangerous and the reason the pup must receive immediate veterinary attention.

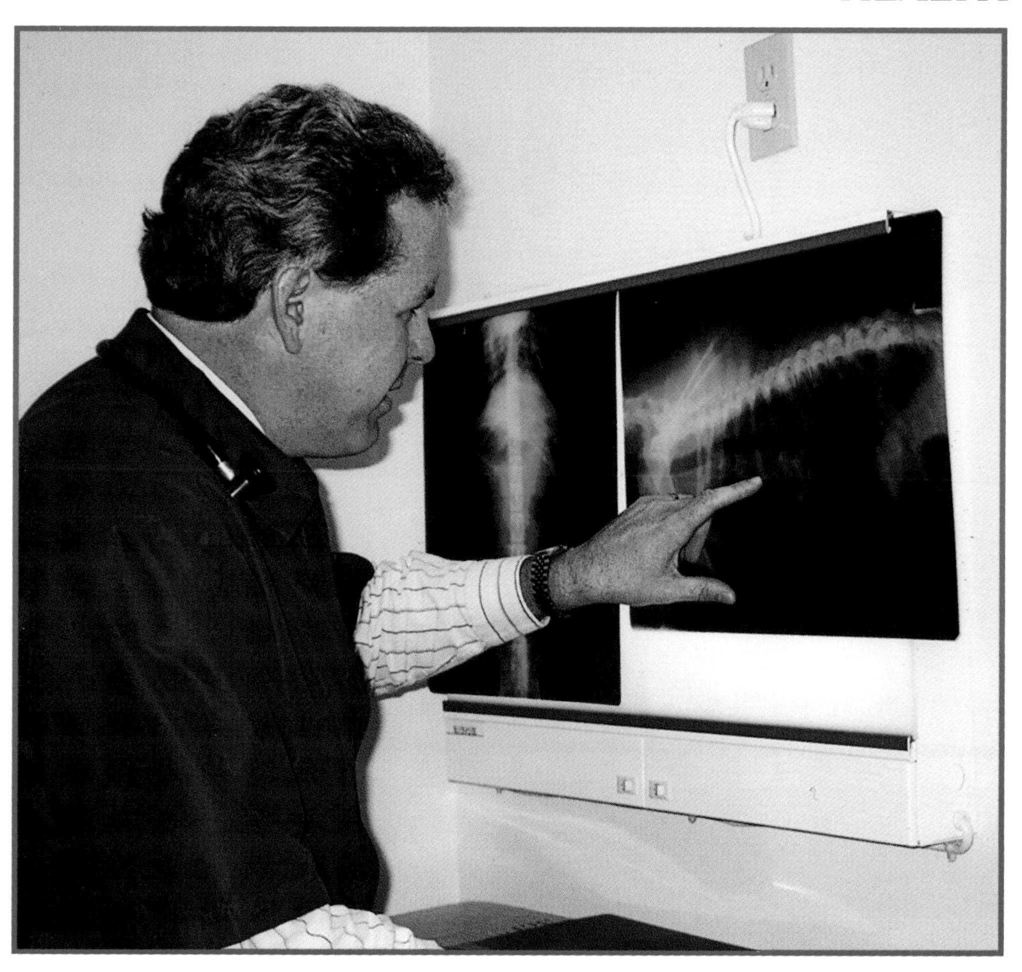

It is a good idea to x-ray the chest and abdomen on any dog hit by a car.

If a broken limb is suspected then try to keep the animal as still as possible. Wrap your pup or dog in a blanket to restrict movement and get him to the veterinarian as soon as possible. Do not move the dog's head so it is tilting backward, as this might result in blood entering the lungs.

Do not let your pup jump up and down from heights, as this can cause considerable shock to the joints. Like all youngsters, puppies do not know when enough is enough, so you must do all their thinking for them.

Provided you apply strict hygiene to all aspects of raising your puppy, and you make daily checks on his physical state, you have done as much as you can to safeguard him during his most vulnerable period. Routine visits to your veterinarian are also recommended, especially while the puppy is under one year of age. The vet may notice something that did not seem important to you.

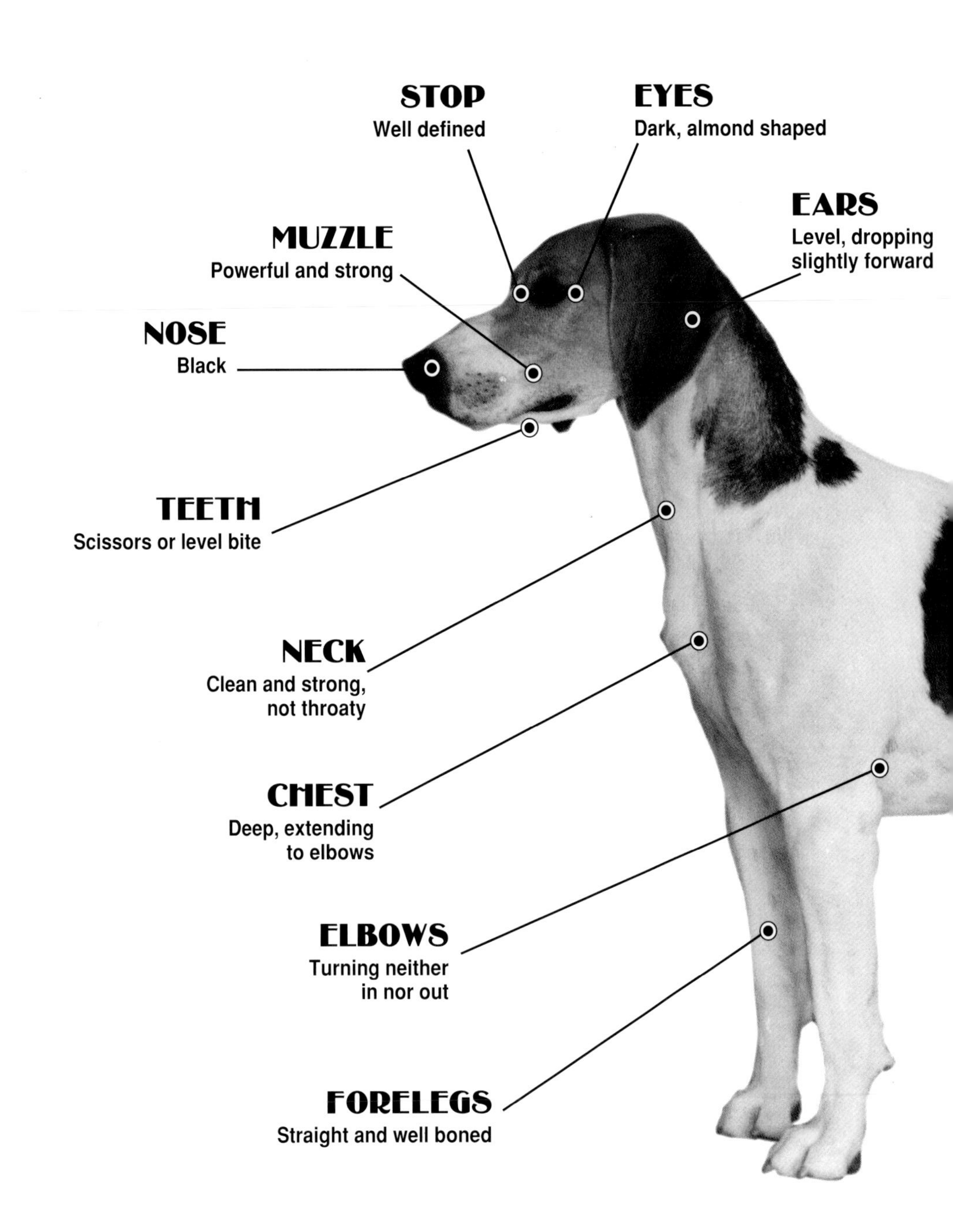

Am. Can. Mex. Int. Ch. Kingbury's Sweet Desert Fire, CD, bred and owned by Donna Smiley-Auborn and co-owned with Kevin Shupenia